Love Yourself

—— TO ——

HEALTH

GIULIANA GIULIANO-MELO

LOVE YOURSELF TO HEALTH

By Giuliana Giuliano-Melo

Copyright © 2018 Giuliana Giuliano-Melo

Transcendent Publishing
PO Box 66202
St. Pete Beach, FL 33736
www.transcendentpublishing.com

ISBN-13: 9781731010117

Printed in the United States of America.

Dedication

When women support other women, miracles happen.

I want to dedicate this to my grandma, Josephine Aiello, who even in spirit supports me. To my mom, who is the vision of faith, forgiveness, integrity, strength and love. To my sister, who never gives up and is the symbol of perseverance. To all of my aunties, cousins and friends who inspire me daily.

A very special thank you to Shanda Trofe. She inspires and supports me and helped bring this vision to life.
I am eternally in appreciation to her.

I also want to dedicate this to all my teachers without whom I would have never birthed this to reality. I especially want to thank Sunny Dawn Johnston who took me under her wing and nurtured me back to health and taught me I am valuable and worthy of love. I want to thank her for being my lighthouse.

CONTENTS

Introduction

Today I am a 54-year-old woman. For forty-six years I was coasting through life. I, like most, had issues with my self-esteem. I was the fat girl. I came from a family where weight was always an issue. I was only five pounds when I was born, but they fattened me up so well that the weight has stayed on my entire life.

In my early teens, my parents would put us on diets to help us lose weight. Even though they were wanting to help, I see now how it fed my not feeling I was good enough, unworthiness, and even though I was very smart, I was always questioning whether or not I was doing something right. I needed approval of my teachers. I just wanted to fit in. I had a desire to be liked.

I was a 'good' girl, as being Italian we were taught that what people thought of us was important. We couldn't bring shame to the family. Being the oldest, along with my parents wanting to teach us responsibility meant learning chores of cleaning the house, cooking, paying bills, and tending to the younger siblings. My mom was very sick with Meniere 's syndrome so at a young age I had to take care of the younger kids. My younger sister was also very sick during her life.

I am the mother, caregiver, and nurturer archetype.

In my group of friends, I also tended to be the social worker. I was the one people came to when they had a problem. I am a great listener. I am sensitive and because of that, I always worried about hurting other people's feelings, so often that I kept my feelings suppressed.

After I graduated from high school in 1982, I left my hometown to go to the city to technical school. I loved the city. Soon after graduation from tech school in '83, I got a job at a major hospital.

In 1985, I met my husband, and in 1998, I had my son. We had many years of unexplained infertility. Going through that played with my emotions. There were extreme highs and lows. However, in 1998 I was given a miracle with the birth of my son.

My son was born blue and need resuscitation, but pinked up within a few minutes. For all intents and purposes, he seemed great and met most milestones on time. But, when he was old enough to go to daycare, the staff realized he had some special needs. I always put my son and my family first. I had worked fulltime until I had my son, and for a few years after up until September 11th, 2001. That is when I realized my son was more important and I went to part-time.

Being sensitive, I had a hard time coping with the issues of having a special son and all that meant. Medicine is my passion but being in a job that never really understood the delicate situation a parent goes through trying to balance work and life just wasn't nourishing my soul. The exchange of energy was: I did a job and got paid. Beyond that, my body was slowly dying. I developed migraines, a pelvic myofascial disorder, type 2 diabetes, and then the big one! Stage 3 peritoneal cancer. I believe I manifested the cancer because I was ignoring what my heart longed for. I worked a job because I made good money. Where I come from, Italians feel strongly that you should get a job and make a decent wage. To have a pension is a badge of honour.

My advice to you is mould your career around your lifestyle, your beliefs, and what your soul longs to do. Not your life around money. I felt safe working in a large hospital for a big corporation, but it didn't serve my highest good. It helped to meet my financial obligations.

The cancer was a huge wakeup call. Looking back I realized the diabetes was a whisper. I didn't listen.

Cancer was scary.

The hardest thing I ever had to do was get up when I thought and felt I was dying, to moving forward with my life instead of sitting in fear. I had to have a very complicated major surgery. I had a total abdominal hysterectomy, an omentectomy, both tubes and ovaries taken out, my appendix removed and 12 lymph nodes taken out. After that, I had six chemotherapy sessions.

I remember lying on the couch, full of chemo, mad at God, and asking, "WHY ME?" And then something shifted. I suddenly thought, "WHY NOT ME? Who the heck am I that I never thought this might happen to me? I am no more special than any other cancer patient before me or after me." And in that instant I knew I had met my soul. I had an inner knowing that it would all be all right.

I had always believed in God having been raised Catholic, but this was deeper. When I reached acceptance of my state of health at the time I was diagnosed, it didn't mean I was resigned to it. It meant I understood it as a part of my path. I awoke to the fact that I had to change my life.

That meant loving myself to health.

The tips and tools in this book are the ones I used and recommend. I suggest taking your time and really sitting with the information in the pages ahead. Intend that you are worth it and create space in your schedule each day to work on an element.

To your health,

How to use the Guide and Journal

- A private daily record of events.
- Meditate beforehand, or sit in quiet reflection of the day to discover what you want to write about.
- Read what you write.
- Write from your heart and get out of your head – what that means is *feel* what it is that you want to say. Don't just *think* it.

This will help you when you say

- You don't have time.
- I don't know what to journal.
- How do I start?
- Help me.

W- what do you want to journal about?
R- review your day
I- internal thoughts and emotions
T- time spent healing
E- end of your day gratitude and reflection

Self-Love

Loving yourself to health
begins with self-love.
It will change your life!

What is Self-Love?

- Self-love is a strong affection for you.
- It is holding yourself dear.
- The regard for your own wellness.

Loving yourself to health begins with self-love. Falling in love with yourself may seem tough to do, but through this course you will learn it is not only possible, but your Divine birthright. It will also change your life. You will learn tools and tips to love yourself to health through acts of self-care.

You may not realize it yet, but self-care is Divine care, for each of us is a piece of the Divine. We are not physical bodies who happen to have souls, but souls embodied, having an earth experience. Yet, in order to learn to love ourselves, we must learn to love the skin we're in. I did, and I'm hoping you will have accomplished the same by the end of this course.

When you learn to love yourself, your life changes in ways you never thought possible. I know, because mine did. I now act, talk, eat, think, like I love myself. I have learned to create boundaries and expect others to treat me with respect.

Now, take a minute to check in with yourself. How do you do that? Place a hand on your heart and breathe mindfully. Breathe in deeply and exhale. Do this a few times. How do you feel? Are you happy? Do you love your life? If the answer is yes, congratulations! This course will add more tools to your toolbox. If the answer is NO, then this course is for you and will change everything!

When you love yourself, you stop the self–sabotage and other destructive behaviours that have kept you stuck. This takes discipline, of course, and you must commit to it and create space each and every day. I have learned...

committed + consistent = SUCCESS

So my friend, DO THE WORK.

I remember when, while walking through some forgiveness work, I called my sister, wanting to share what was going on. Her response: that I couldn't expect her to always be there for me. The words stung, but they were true. I had just learned an important lesson the hard way, and that lesson was: At the end of each day, you and God are all you've got.

> *Self-love is so important because when you find yourself crying in your bed, all alone, whether it is at four a.m. or four p.m., who is going to be there for you? YOU! You must be the one to pick yourself up and dig deep down for the strength to move on.*

Practicing Self-Love

- Loving yourself despite the thing(s) you don't like about your body. This alone can be a game- changer. I know, because I used to hate my body. I used to be so mean to me.

- Being your authentic self

- Taking off the masks that you are hiding behind because of fear of judgement

- Stopping the bullying self-talk

- Creating healthy boundaries

- Taking time to experience JOY every day

- Creating space in your day just for you

- Create a life you love

- Taking care of your mind, body and spirit

- Eating good food to nourish you and heal you

- Treating the body as a temple – after all, it's where your soul is housed during this lifetime!

- Taking time to connect to Creator/God/Universe

- Taking time for self-care

- Getting physical exercise

- Self-acceptance

- Self-pleasure

- Honouring and respecting yourself

- Empowerment

- Valuing yourself

- Trusting yourself

- Forgiving yourself

Self-Love Affirmations

My body heals with loving words

I am healthy.

I am whole, perfect and complete.

I tell my body to accept healing and health.

I am accepting health in my body.

I talk to all of my cells to heal my body and mind.

I am health.

I am attracting people and the highest information that will help me live a healthy life.

I am open to releasing all my unhealthy thoughts.

My health is very important to me.

I intend to live in optimum health.

I see myself healthy and whole.

I allow my body to heal itself.

My body is healing my whole being.

I release my past and leave it behind me.

I am open to releasing unhealthy people.

My DNA is programmed for optimum health.

I forgive because it is good for my health.

I tell my body thank you for carrying my soul.

It feels so good to be me.

I am so happy and grateful for this beautiful body.

Create your own affirmations:

_____

_____

_____

_____

_____

_____

_____

_____

_____

_____

_____

_____

_____

_____

_____

_____

_____

_____

_____

_____

_____

Twelve Commandments to Love Yourself

By Louise Hay

Are you wondering how to love yourself? I have found that there is only one thing that heals every problem, and that is: *truly loving yourself.* When people start to love themselves more each day, it's amazing how their lives get better. They feel better. They get the jobs they want. They have the money they need. Their relationships either improve, or the negative ones dissolve and new ones begin.

Loving yourself is a wonderful adventure; it's like learning to fly. Imagine if we all had the power to fly at will? How exciting it would be! Let's begin to love ourselves now.

Here are 12 Commandments to help you learn how to love yourself:

1. Stop All Criticism

Criticism never changes a thing. Refuse to criticize yourself. Accept yourself exactly as you are. Everybody changes. When you criticize yourself, your changes are negative. When you approve of yourself, your changes are positive.

2. Forgive Yourself

Let the past go. You did the best you could at the time with the understanding, awareness, and knowledge that you had. Now you are growing and changing, and you will live life differently.

3. Don't Scare Yourself

Stop terrorizing yourself with your thoughts. It's a dreadful way to live. Find a mental image that gives you pleasure, and immediately switch your scary thought to a pleasure thought.

4. Be Gentle and Kind and Patient

Be gentle with yourself. Be kind to yourself. Be patient with yourself as you learn the new ways of thinking. Treat yourself as you would someone you really loved.

5. Be Kind to Your Mind

Self-hatred is only hating your own thoughts. Don't hate yourself for having the thoughts. Gently change your thoughts.

6. Praise Yourself

Criticism breaks down the inner spirit. Praise builds it up. Praise yourself as much as you can. Tell yourself how well you are doing with every little thing.

7. Support Yourself

Find ways to support yourself. Reach out to friends and allow them to help you. It is being strong to ask for help when you need it.

8. Be Loving to Your Negatives

Acknowledge that you created them to fulfill a need. Now you are finding new, positive ways to fulfill those needs. So lovingly release the old negative patterns.

9. Take Care of Your Body

Learn about nutrition. What kind of fuel does your body need in order to have optimum energy and vitality? Learn about exercise. What kind of exercise do you enjoy? Cherish and revere the temple you live in.

10. Do Mirror Work

Look into your eyes often. Express this growing sense of love you have for yourself. Forgive yourself while looking into the mirror. Talk to your parents while looking into the mirror. Forgive them, too. At least once a day, say, I love you, I really love you!

11. Love Yourself . . . Do It Now

Don't wait until you get well, or lose the weight, or get the new job, or find the new relationship. Begin now—and do the best you can.

12. Have Fun

Remember the things that gave you joy as a child. Incorporate them into your life now. Find a way to have fun with everything you do. Let yourself express the joy of living. Smile. Laugh. Rejoice, and the Universe rejoices with you!

Self-Care

"As I loved and respected myself more, I stopped worrying about how much others liked or approved of me. I stopped doing things to be liked. This created space for me to be more authentic, less defensive, and more my genuine self. When you have your own approval and acceptance, you start caring less about other people's opinion of you and living a life that's aligned with your own values."

~Aska Kolton

What is Self-Care?

Self–care is the energy with which we take actions to care for our mind, body and spirit. It is also the energy of our emotions. Self-love is like the lotus flower that blossoms when we participate in acts of self-care. It is our heart, opening like a rose.

Take the time to do the things you need to in order to feel in harmony with life. Honour your spirit. Let yourself off the hook for things in the past. Self- care is learning to forgive yourself and all others, and to always reach for your highest good.

Most of us – especially those of us who are mothers - have learned to take care of everyone else, often at our own expense.

But how can we take care of anyone else when our tank is empty? My late friend and accountability partner, Vicky M. and I spent hundreds of hours healing together and almost every single time she asked me, "Giuliana, is your love tank empty?"

Her words would stop me in my tracks. Vicki was right. I was depleted. I was running on empty. I used to give to the point of resentment. Through our mentor and each other, I learned to become a better receiver and never give in "obligation vibration." It feels so much better now!

Most of us say *yes* when we should be saying *no*. We have learned that taking time for ourselves is selfish. Now I know that it is not only okay, but absolutely necessary, to take time just for you, your health, and your life! When you feel good you have more energy to give to everyone else, whether they be colleagues or friends, family members or pets. Self-care is the act of filling your cup or "love tank" to overflowing and then helping others from that overflow.

Self-care means checking in with yourself each day. When a baby cries, you check what it needs. Is it food? Water? A change of scenery? Fun? Perhaps the baby needs rest or sleep. In the same way, you must ask yourself: "What do I need right now?" Listen to what you get, let your intuition guide you. Self-care is a key to healing.

There Are 8 Areas of Self-Care:

1. **Physical** - bathing, brushing teeth, washing hair and paying attention to the needs of the body. Diet and exercise, getting enough sleep. It also means maintaining health insurance and making yearly appointments with the following:

   - Doctor

   - Dentist

   - Optometrist/ophthalmologist

   - Gynaecologist (women), Urologist (men)

2. **Emotional** - How do you handle yourself when you are angry, upset or not feeling well mentally?

3. **Spiritual** - these are activities, regardless of religion, that allow you to connect with Source.

4. **Professional** - Are you working in a job you love? If not, why not?

5. **Environmental** - this is where you live (this is one of the most important factors as you cannot heal in the same environment that made you sick).

6. **Financial** - What are your beliefs around money? Do you tend to save it, or spend it? Most importantly, do you respect it? Money affords us experiences. We need to trust

that there will always be an endless supply that we can tap into at all times. *Remember, money is energy.*

7. **Social** - What do you do to connect with others and have fun? When is retreating healthy, and when is it cause for alarm? Do you tend to isolate, as I once did? Isolation can be good when it is done to tune and maintain your own energy; it is not healthy when you avoid others out of fear.

8. **Personal** - Who are you? Not your name, but who are you *really?* Strip back the labels. Are you still seeking external validation, or do you feel it is time to go within and be your own guru?

10 Steps to Self-Care

1. Love yourself
2. Say what you mean and mean what you say
3. Trust your intuition
4. Always chase your dreams
5. Learn to say NO
6. Say YES (to love, fun, anything else that's aligned with our highest good)
7. Let go of things that are not in your control
8. Stay away from drama and negativity
9. Forgive all things in your past, forgive yourself.
10. Worry about NOTHING

What act(s) of self-care will you commit to practicing daily? How will you add it in?

_____

_____

_____

_____

_____

_____

_____

_____

_____

_____

_____

_____

_____

_____

_____

_____

_____

_____

_____

_____

_____

_____

_____

_____

_____

_____

Sign your commitment: X _____ **Date:** _____

Exercise: Go on a Date with Yourself

Taking yourself out is a great act of self-care. It is empowering and liberating.

- Decide when to go on a date with yourself. Make room in your calendar just for you.
- Go somewhere different each time. Use this time to do something new and different. Step outside your box. Stretch yourself.

Some date ideas are:

1. Massage
2. Exercise
3. Nature walk
4. Movie
5. Meal out
6. Go for a drive and notice the scenery
7. The options are endless.

Your date ideas:

_____

_____

_____

_____

_____

_____

_____

_____

Record your date here...

_____

_____

_____

_____

_____

_____

_____

_____

_____

_____

_____

_____

_____

_____

_____

_____

_____

_____

_____

_____

_____

_____

_____

_____

_____

_____

_____

_____

_____

_____

Intention

"Where **Attention** goes
energy flows;
Where **Intention** goes
energy flows! "
~James Redfield

Time to Take Action!

There are three big steps to heal your life.

They are:

1. **Connect to Source, God, Creator, and Universe** - whatever you call it – each and every day.
2. **Forgive yourself and all others.** We forgive because we deserve it.
3. **LOVE YOURSELF.**

Now we will move into action. With open hearts, let's use the power of self-love to make a promise and set an intention. This helps us stay strong and create the reality we wish. Let's no longer settle, but instead bring in our deepest desires. We are worth it!

INTENTION: speak your truth, receive guidance and trust your inner wisdom and power to make a promise and keep it. Promise to LOVE YOURSELF.

In the space below, write down what you are going to do over these three weeks to love yourself to health.

1. _____
2. _____
3. _____
4. _____
5. _____
6. _____
7. _____
8. _____
9. _____

Self-Love Promise

Let's make a Self-Love promise because we are worth it!

A self-love promise is a sacred contract you make with you and your spirit and your soul. It is made from love. It has no judgement. This is a vow you make with yourself and you keep it. It helps empower you by giving you the strength to choose love for yourself in every situation.

PROMISE: I, _____, hereby promise myself that I will take care of my mind, body and spirit, by doing a daily spiritual practice, by eating and drinking healthy foods and by thinking healthy thoughts. I will move my body. I will release old pain, shame and guilt because I deserve to be healthy and strong!

I love me. I love me. I love me! Amen! And so it is.

Signed X _____ Date: _____

Daily Spiritual Practice:

- Gratitude- take time each day to be grateful- say *Thank you, thank you, thank you!*

- Mindful breathing – inhale deeply to the count of four, then exhale slowly, again, counting to four. Connect with your breath.

- Pray in a way that feels good for you: thinking positive thoughts and wishing others well are a form of prayer. Hug a friend. Prayer is a vibration. It is a feeling. Prayer is talking to the Divine.

- Meditate - listen in. Close your eyes and be still.

- Protect and maintain your energy by envisioning yourself in a Divine white light bubble of protection (if you work with Archangel Michael you can envision his blue light around you).

- Ground yourself to Mother Earth by imagining roots growing from your feet deep into the soil and anchoring you like a tree (see page 29).

- Be open and receptive to receive your blessings by saying this aloud with outstretched arms.

- Each day, ask the Universe, How may I be of service today?

- Ask the Universe to guide your steps and to help you on your path.

- Ask your guardian angels for help with whatever it is that you need.

- Self-love affirmations (See list at the end of this workbook).

- Take a "sacred bath" each day by clearing your energy with a sea salt or Epsom salt bath. You can also take a visual-ization shower by imaging all the yuck of the day being washed away.

- Invoking angels to help you. Ask them in. Just say out loud or in your head, "Angels please help me."

Each day, the moment I awake, I say…

"Thank you, thank you, thank you, God, that I am alive." Then I may say my prayers or meditate. This takes only a few minutes, but it makes a HUGE difference. Promise yourself you'll do it every day for these three weeks. Twenty-one days is all it takes to form a habit. You will begin to notice the difference and then you will never want to stop.

Create Your Daily Spiritual Practice

_____

_____

_____

_____

_____

_____

_____

_____

_____

_____

_____

_____

_____

_____

_____

_____

_____

_____

_____

_____

_____

_____

_____

_____

_____

_____

_____

_____

_____

_____

_____

Meditation: Create Your Day with Intention

Feet flat on floor, close your eyes, put your hand on your heart.
Connect to your breath.

Begin by placing a hand on your heart
and connect with your breath.

Breathe in deeply and mindfully. Exhale and relax your body.

Imagine white light coming in through your crown chakra at the
top of your head. Allow it to run through your body, out the
bottom of your feel and deep into Mother Earth, to anchor and
ground you. Then imagine it flowing all the way up again and
out through your heart chakra, until you visualize yourself
surrounded in a bubble of white light.

Affirm: *I am a child of the light. I am love. I have within me
deep wisdom to carry me through this day with ease and Grace.
I am a powerful co-creator with Source. I can manifest all my
dreams. I am safe. I am Divinely supported at all times.*

Thank you, and so it is.

Breathe dear one. You are love.

***This meditation is the one I created from the book *111 Morning
Meditations: Create Your Day With Intention.*

Create Your Own Meditation:

_____

_____

_____

_____

_____

_____

_____

_____

_____

_____

_____

_____

_____

_____

_____

_____

_____

_____

_____

_____

_____

_____

_____

_____

_____

_____

_____

_____

_____

Ground & Connect with Mother Earth

Go outside. With bare feet in the grass ask Mother Earth to cleanse your energy and ground yourself by imagining big roots growing from the bottoms of your feet deep into the earth. Allow her to take all the yucky energy from you. Walk in the sand. Hug a tree. Listen to the birdies. Fill up with the sunshine. Feel the rain on your face. Honour Mother Earth and nature. This is how we connect to the planet and the energy of her. Allow her energy to envelope you and nurture you by sending all fear, pain and sadness to be dissolved into the earth to be replaced with more love. Nature is healing. This is a huge act of self-love. Then send Love to Mother Earth. Thank her for keeping us safe.

Write a letter of gratitude to Mother Earth:

_____

_____

_____

_____

_____

_____

_____

_____

_____

_____

_____

_____

_____

Exercise: Write Yourself a Love Letter

Speak Kindly to your body. This is the letter I wrote to mine. You can follow it to do yours.

Dear beautiful Body of mine,

I am so, so sorry. I am sorry for the all the ways I have ever hurt you. I am sorry for trying to detach from you. I am sorry for hurting you. I am sorry for betraying you. I am sorry for hating you. I am sorry for poisoning you. Especially with all the chemo!! I am sorry for maligning you and calling you names! I am sorry for being ashamed of you and wanting to be someone else. I am sorry for having put you in dangerous positions! I am sorry for all the ways I let you down. I am sorry for underestimating you. I am sorry for fearing you and your power. I am sorry for not acknowledging your deep wisdom. I am sorry for not letting you lead the way. I am sorry for closing you off to receiving. I am sorry for allowing others to harm you. I am sorry for shutting you down to pleasure and love. I am sorry for denying you. I am sorry for shaming you. I am sorry for allowing others to shame you. I am sorry for alternately pushing you too hard and not encouraging you harder. I am sorry for not trusting you. I am sorry for bullying you. I am sorry for not listening to your protests or signals. I am sorry for not believing in you. I am sorry for taking over your journey. I am sorry for labeling your feelings as bad or wrong. I am sorry for thinking you were broken and needed to be fixed. I am sorry I didn't love you more. I am sorry I didn't tell you how much I appreciate you. I am sorry I hid you. I am sorry you are hurting. I am sorry for all the times you felt shut down. I am sorry for trusting others opinions more than hearing what you really need. I am sorry I let you down.

I am so, so sorry. Please forgive me. Thank you so very much for my life, my son, my pleasure, my ability to feel, hear, see and know everything - love, compassion, peace, joy, ecstasy, bliss, sorrow, grief, rage. Thank you for my ability to walk, run, see, smell, kiss, taste, make love, hug, dance! PLAY! Thank you for so much more that you are, do, feel and sense. Thank you for giving me this amazing beautiful human life.

I love you. I love you. I love you. I love you. I love you.

Loving you through eternity, I am so glad I woke up!!

~Me

Your turn...

Dear _____,

_____

_____

_____

_____

_____

_____

_____

_____

_____

_____

Sacred Bath Time

Water is much more than something we swim or wash our bodies in. It is liquid light, with powerful physical and energetic healing and cleansing properties. Through my Goddess work, I learned to use these properties each night to clear and cleanse my energy of everything I have absorbed each day. I love to use Himalayan bath salts or Epsom salts (if you feel guided, you may also use essential oils to make the pink Himalayan bath salts smell good). The salts help remove unwanted energies that we pick up during the day. It clears the energetic and physical bodies at the same time.

Soak with the intention of clearing all that no longer serves you. If you do not have a tub, you can rub salt on your body in your shower. It is all in the intention. You can also soak your feet in a clean pail of water and salt.

Take note of how you feel before your sacred bath time.

Take note of how you feel afterward.

Journal your experience here:

_____

_____

_____

_____

_____

_____

_____

_____

_____

_____

INTENTION

Mirror Work

Mirror Work is when we look into our eyes in a mirror and proclaim, "I love you, (your name). I really love you. I love you. I deeply love you."

What do you see when you look into your eyes? If feelings come up, allow them. Welcome them. Laugh, cry but say the I LOVE YOU.

If you find you can't hold the gaze for long, that's okay. Keep trying until you can. Fall in love with yourself. Let her off the hook. Forgive her. Affirm: I am loved. I am lovable. I am love.

As you complete this task each day, thank yourself. This seemingly simple act of self-care is actually the most Divine, for it is you connecting with your soul which is connected to the SOURCE of all there is and ever shall be.

Allow all the feelings to arise in you and within you and allow them out by journaling. There is no judgement here. I remember when I first started this, I would say all kinds of nasty things to myself. Slowly it shifted and now I can say I LOVE YOU to me.

What came up for you?

_____

_____

_____

_____

_____

_____

Letting Go

Write and Rip or Write and Burn Technique

Write out your thoughts. Go for fifteen minutes on anything bothering you. Set a powerful intention to let it go and ask your Divine Team of God, Angels and guides to help you transmute that pain energy as you burn or tear the paper. And so it is. Always burn in a safe container and outside if you can, or in the sink.

_____

_____

_____

_____

_____

_____

_____

_____

_____

_____

_____

_____

_____

_____

_____

_____

_____

_____

_____

_____

_____

_____

INTENTION

Releasing with Letters

Write letters to release built up energy. The letters are not to be sent. This is a very powerful process, which allows you to express your truth, and then when you burn them or tear them you allow the hurt, anger and pain to be transmuted back to love.

Write a letter to your inner child:

_____

_____

_____

_____

_____

_____

_____

_____

_____

_____

_____

_____

_____

_____

_____

_____

_____

_____

_____

_____

_____

_____

Write a letter to someone you're upset with:

_____

_____

_____

_____

_____

_____

_____

_____

_____

_____

_____

_____

_____

_____

_____

_____

_____

_____

_____

_____

_____

_____

_____

_____

_____

_____

Word of the Year- Setting Intentions

Choosing a word to guide your year will help set a powerful intention and tells the Universe to guide you. Your soul will guide you and you will experience the magic and mystery in the journey of life.

I first started using words to guide my year in 2015. My word was Grace. Indeed, I did experience the Grace of God in everything.

Then in 2016, my word was future. 2017 was expansion and it was tough. This year my words are Abundance, Integrate and Respond. I also felt guided to add boundaries.

You may be asking how do we choose a word? Well I sat with my spirit. I allowed my intuition to guide me. It is one of the most powerful experiences and way better than making resolutions that never work.

Ask yourself what you need. Right now and going into the New Year, what do you need? My word almost always forms from that question. If that word doesn't immediately resonate with you, check with a thesaurus and see if one of the words associated with it does. Ask yourself what qualities can help you achieve that thing that you need.

Make a Word List. Write down all of the words that are calling out to you right now. They can be random words, don't overthink it, just let the words release and flow out.

Write down your goals. If you are someone that likes to make a lot of goals or resolutions, write them all down and then see if there's a theme that's connecting them. Maybe your word needs to be "motivation" so you can tackle all the things on your list, or "fit" to inspire you to move more.

Who do you want to be? It's common to want to turn over a new leaf – I know I can name several qualities I want to cultivate within myself. What qualities or traits do you want to bring into your life? Let your word inspire you to be that thing.

Don't overthink it. My word sometimes takes me awhile to figure it out. I usually start thinking about it in the beginning of December and sometimes it doesn't come to me until I'm halfway through January. Your word will feel right. You'll know it when you find it.

48 Word Suggestions

Here are some words that might resonate with you! The first 10 are ones that I personally have chosen as intentions over the past few years. Energy flows where your attention goes. This is a powerful way to INTEND your year.

1	Grace
2	Future
3	More
4	Life
5	Abundance
6	Integrate
7	Respond
8	Boundaries
9	Illumination
10	Love
11	Expansion
12	Courage
13	Truth

14   Forgive
15   Healing
16   Mindfulness
17   Patience
18   Transformation
19   Calm
20   Intention
21   Joy
22   Light
23   Quiet
24   Adventure
25   Yes
26   Connection
27   Organized
28   Spirituality
29   Passion
30   Hope
31   Nourish
32   Nurture
33   Enlightened
34   Freedom
35   Uniqueness
36   Thrive
37   Progress
38   Appreciate
39   Intuition
40   Release
41   Explore
42   Breathe
43   Wellness
44   Emergence
45   Permission
46   Present
47   Glowing
48   Recovery

What's your word of the year? _____

What does it mean to you?

_____
_____
_____
_____
_____
_____
_____
_____
_____
_____
_____
_____
_____
_____
_____
_____
_____
_____
_____
_____
_____
_____
_____
_____
_____
_____
_____
_____
_____
_____

Fill up with fun ideas

Do something fun every day!

- Colouring
- Comedy
- Cooking
- Dancing
- Music
- Camping
- Meditation
- Singing
- Playing
- Gardening
- Sun-tanning
- Visiting a friend
- Shopping
- Hugging
- Watching movies
- Drawing
- Swimming

Your fun ideas:

_____

_____

_____

_____

_____

_____

Just for fun...

Created by Lori Farrell of Twisted Art Designs

Goals

"You have to speak your dream out loud."

~ Kelly Corrigan

Goals And Dreams - Vision Boards

Benefits of Creating a Vision Board

1. It Brings CLARITY to Dreams, allowing you to rewire your brain.

2. It allows us to tap into a greater level of AWARENESS; you will discover that all the answers are within us. Self-doubt will not succeed.

3. It provides INCENTIVES, great reminders of what your goals are.

4. It harnesses the power of the law of attraction.

How to create a vision board:

- Gather together your old magazines and cut out people, places and things you wish to see, be and do
- Purchase a board of some kind or sheet of construction paper, glue, scissors, tape, markers, pencils and pens
- Purchase stickers that are fun
- Set an intention or use one of the words provided in the word for the year area
- Have a photo of yourself for the middle of the board
- When you are ready, assemble your photos and words in organized areas on the board.
- Make sure you have a quiet space to create in.
- Turn on some gentle music.
- Light a candle safely away from the papers.

- Pray or meditate on what you would like to bring in this year.
- Decide if it going to be a messy board or a more organized board.
- Invoke your Divine Team of support (God, angels, guides and goddesses) in to help you.
- Put it all together in a way that feels good for you.

After Creating Your Vision Board

Once you've created your vision board, place it in an area that you see every day. Many people like to notice their vision board near their nightstand or other place that they look at first thing in the morning.

After a time, and to avoid "not really seeing" your vision board, make it a habit of sitting with your board at least once a week. Simply take ten minutes to look at your board, reflect on why you specifically chose those images, and revisit the feelings of happiness and gratitude of eventually having those desires manifest in your life.

Not only is a vision board a wonderful reminder of what you truly want in life, it's a **powerful motivator and catalyst for achieving your goals**. It is also a special gift you've given to yourself, so treat it like it is sacred.

Follow through with your self-care plans and focus on your goals.

Visions ...

... and Dreams

Exercise: Answering Your Heart's Calling

Close your eyes, tap into your higher self. Ask your angels to stand behind you and help you calm your mind and then go within to your heart and ask what it is that you need. Imagine your heart opening like the petals on a rose.

What does your heart need?

_____

_____

_____

_____

_____

_____

_____

_____

_____

_____

_____

_____

_____

_____

_____

_____

_____

_____

_____

_____

_____

_____

_____

_____

Body, Mind & Soul

"An Empty Lantern provides no light! Self-love and self-care are the fuel that allows your light to shine brightly!"
~Unknown

Learning to love my body

Once I learned we are energy, everything began to shift for me. I realized the fat I carried was old energy that I could release. I have been digging deep to heal my old wounds. I had to heal my inner child and become an empowered woman. I had to love my body. I began to look at it as energy and I now talk, act, eat, think as someone who loves herself.

I have learned about vibrational eating, which means to select high quality, high vibration food. Whole foods. I had to learn to eat from a neutral vibration. I also learned to pay attention to the emotions I was eating in my food. Was I eating with shame and guilt or was I happy and pleased with my choices?

How are you feeling when you eat your food? Take your time and notice how you are feeling when you are eating.

What pain is in your pounds?

_____

_____

_____

_____

_____

_____

_____

_____

_____

_____

_____

Self-Care Ideas for the Body

1. Breathe deeply and mindfully.

2. Pay attention to the signs your body is sending. Scan your body from head to toe, noticing any pain or discomfort. Go within and ask yourself, what is causing the pain?

3. Dance it out – move that body!

4. Stretch or do yoga.

5. Get some exercise.

6. Practice stillness.

7. Get some sunshine.

8. Ground with Mother Earth. Go barefoot in the grass. Walk through the forest. Hug a tree. Smell the flowers.

9. Eat regularly

10. Eat healthy

11. Get regular medical care

12. Get massages

13. Get enough sleep

14. Once per year go somewhere you have never been before

Self-Care Ideas for the Mind

1. Start a gratitude journal. Write down 3 things or experiences that you are grateful for. Read often.

2. Bring out your inner child to play. Sing, dance, laugh, draw

or colour at least once a day.

3. Delete negative people from your social media and personal life.

4. Do your affirmation work. Refer to the list included in this workbook.

5. Change your thoughts, change your life.

6. Learn to say NO – no is a complete sentence

7. Take regular social media breaks

Self-Care Ideas for the Soul

1. Practice kindness. Open a door, smile, offer a compliment or buy someone a coffee.

2. Check in with your emotions. Sit quietly and take note of how you are feeling in this moment. Hand on heart. What is coming up?

3. Choose who you spend your time with today. Hang out with positivity peeps and not energy vampires (those who suck your energy dry).

4. Pet an animal. If you don't have one perhaps ask a friend to hold and pet their animal or volunteer at the Animal Shelter in your area.

5. Pray. pray in a way that feels good to you. Prayer is not only when we put our hands together and talk to God. Prayer Is also thinking positive thoughts and sending them to a friend. It is hugging a friend and wishing them well. It is saying "drive safe".

When you help someone and when you forgive, that is a prayer.

This is a prayer that I wrote…

Angel Prayer for Friendship

Dear Angels,

I come to you now for my friends that I have on my heart
today.
Please bring joy to decrease their sadness.
Please bring hope when they feel lost
Please heal their body when they are sick
Please fill them with light when they are in the dark
Please calm their brain when in anxiety
Please soothe their soul when in grief and dry their tears when
they cry.
Please help them feel loved when alone.
Please bring comfort when in pain
Please bring strength when weak
Please guard and guide
And most of all,
help them to know the Grace of God
all the days of their lives.
For this I pray.
And so it is.
Amen.

Faith

All you need is faith the size of a mustard seed.

1 Mathew 17:20

Faith and belief in a Higher Power as an Anchor in my self-love practice

I believe we are love. We come from love and we return to love.

When we connect with love daily, we can't help but love our selves more. We feel

connected to Source and to the highest energy there is.

I am firmly rooted in Catholicism and with God. I have an expanded awareness now of the Universe.

My favourite prayers:

The Hail Mary Prayer

Hail Mary, full of grace.

Our Lord is with thee.

Blessed art thou among women, and blessed is the
fruit of thy womb, Jesus.

Holy Mary, Mother of God, pray for us sinners,
now and at the hour of our death.

Amen.

The Lord's Prayer

Our Father who art in heaven,

hallowed be thy name.

Thy kingdom come.

Thy will be done

on earth as it is in heaven.

Give us this day our daily bread,

and forgive us our trespasses,

as we forgive those who trespass against us,

and lead us not into temptation,

but deliver us from evil.

For thine is the kingdom,

and the power, and the glory,

for ever and ever.

Amen.

Guardian Angel Prayer

Angel of God,

my guardian dear,

to whom God's love commits me here,

ever this day,

be at my side

to light and guard,

to rule and guide.

Amen.

Working with the Angelic Realm

Learning to love myself included my recognizing my own Divinity with being spirit embodied. I also learned of Angels who help us. This is a chart of the realms of the angels.

The Angelic Realm / Spiritual Hierarchy

The 9 orders of angelic beings (1 being the highest order)

The First Sphere — angels who serve as heavenly counsellors

1 – SERAPHIM

2 – CHERUBIM

3 – THRONES

The Second Sphere — angels who work as heavenly governors

4 – DOMINIONS

5 – VIRTUES

6 – POWERS

The Third Sphere — angels who function as heavenly messengers

7 – PRINCIPALITIES

8 – ARCHANGELS

9 – ANGELS

Guardian Angels

Guardian angels are given to us from the moment we are born until the day we return to heaven. They never leave us. We are their only assignment. Because of Divine free will, we must ASK for assistance. Then we must be open and ready to receive the help. We must allow it and surrender and trust that the help will arrive.

Psalm 91:11 New Living Translation (NLT)

"For he will order his angels to protect you wherever you go."

Archangels

This is the specific realm of angels I work with:

Ariel - Archangel of Prosperity

Colour: pale pink

Name means: Lion or Lioness of God

Helps us with: all animals and their care, the earth and making sure we are provided for in terms of all necessities of life. Food, water and shelter.

Affirm: I will be taken care of. I only have to ask. I deserve help. I am safe.

Azrael - Archangel of Death and Grieving

Colour: creamy white

Name means: Whom God helps

Helps us with: grief, death and bereavement

Affirm: Love never dies. It only changes forms. My loved one is safe in LOVE.

Chamuel - Archangel of Unconditional Love and Adoration

Colour: pink

Name means: He who sees or seeks God

Helps us with: self-love, building and strengthening relationships with yourself and others, career, world peace and seeking a soul mate.

Affirm: I am worthy of love for I am made from pure love.

Gabriel - the Archangel of Communication

Colour: white

Name means: God is my strength

Gabriel's energy resonates male and female. He helps with writing, journalism, TV and radio work, child conception and infertility. Gabriel is the messenger angel and he is the one who proclaimed Jesus birth. He was also the one who told Mary she was pregnant.

Affirm: I speak my truth with love. I am safe to speak my truth. I speak my truth with kindness.

Haniel - Archangel of Intuition, Imagination and Emotions

Colour: pale blue

Name means: Glory of God

Helps us with: living our highest best good in our life. Ask her to help you when you want help to discover your gifts.

Affirm: I trust Source to guide me. I follow my intuition

Jophiel - Archangel of Beauty and Creativity

Colour: yellow

Names means : beauty of God

Helps us with: beauty, creativity and art

She is the patron archangel of artists. She helps us clear clutter. She helps bring more beauty into all areas of our life. She helps us look and dress beautiful.

Affirm: I choose to see the beauty that surrounds me. I am creative.

Metatron - Archangel of life

Colour is violet and green

Name means: "one who guards" or "one who serves behind God's throne"

Brother to Sandalphon. These are the only two angels ever to have been in human form. Archangel Metraton was the prophet Enoch and Archangel Sandalphon was the prophet Elijah.

Helps with: prioritization and teaches esoteric wisdom. He helps guard the tree of life and writes down all the good deeds people do on earth as well as heaven. These are all written in the Book of life, also known as the Akashic records.

Affirm: I am divine light. The more good I do, the higher my vibration.

Michael – Archangel of Protection

Colour: blue

Name means: He who is like God

He is the angel of courage, protection, guidance and strength. He helps with maintaining our energy and protecting us as we journey. He also helps with motivation, faith, energy and releasing fear. His colour vibration is electric blue. He carries a sword and shield that are both made of light. His sword helps cut away cords of fear and energetic attachments that no longer serve you.

Affirm: I am safe. All is well. I am courageous.

Raphael - Archangel of Healing

Colour: emerald green

His name means: God has healed

He is the archangel who helps us eliminate unhealthy patterns and habits. He helps those who do healing work and helps find lost pets. When you require healing, visualize yourself being bathed in his emerald green energy.

Affirm: I accept healing now. I am open to healing my life. I am ready to heal my soul.

Raziel - Angel of Tree of Life, Keeper of Secrets, Angel of Mysteries

Colour: Rainbow colors

Name means: "Secret of God" because he works so closely with God that he knows all of the secrets of the universe, and how it operates.

Helps with: Raziel can help you to understand esoteric material and increase your ability to see, hear, know and feel Divine guidance. Alchemy, divine magic and manifesting. Patron Angel of Law Makers and Lawyers.

Affirm: I am Divine flow. I am in perfect timing.

Raguel - Archangel of Justice, Fairness and Harmony

Colour: Pale blue

Name means: Friend of God

Also known as the angel of speech and will help speakers when asked.

Affirm: I attract beautiful experiences. All is in Divine order.

Sandalphon - Archangel of Music

Colour: Turquoise

Name means: together and co-brother

He is the brother of Metatron. He was the prophet Elijah.

Helps as the intercessor of prayers between humans and God. He helps determine the gender of a coming child, and acts as a patron to musicians. He helps us select music that helps soothe and heal. He helps connect our energy to the Divine. He helps us live in integrity and speak our truth.

Affirm: My prayers are always heard and answered for my highest best good.

Uriel - Archangel of Illumination

Colour: red

Name means: God is my light or fire of God

Helps with: wisdom, inspiration, motivation and truth, making decisions, learning new information, solving problems and resolving conflict.

Affirm: I trust my path will present itself to me.

Archangel Zadkiel - Archangel of Forgiveness

Colour: purple

Name means: Righteousness of God

Helps with: forgiveness work, mercy, benevolence, freedom, tolerance and diplomacy

Affirm: Everything is working out for my highest good. I deserve forgiveness.

There are other beautiful energies that I invoke each day. To invoke is to ask and invite into your life. These are some that I want to share with you...

Jesus - Forgiveness

Son of God. Greatest teacher there is. He helps us with our forgiveness work. He loves us so much and helps all who call upon Him. He sees us through the eyes of love and as the children of God we are.

I have always had an intimate relationship with Jesus. I was raised Catholic. Catholicism is still a big part of who I am. I recognize Jesus for what he did for my soul and for mankind. I am forgiven because He died for me. I am loved and live in the knowing that nothing I have ever done or will do won't be forgiven.

Forgiveness is a great act of self-love. When I think of His suffering and His death on the cross, I cry. My soul weeps, for He loves us so. Regardless of any religion, Jesus loves all who calls upon Him for help. I reflect on His journey and I sit in deep reverence and gratitude. Invite Jesus in. He awaits your request. He is a loving, kind and non-judgmental energy.

He also helps with any father issues you may have. The gift of forgiveness frees you from the burdens of the past. Jesus teaches us we forgive because we deserve peace.

Who do you need to forgive?

_____

_____

_____

_____

_____

_____

Holy Spirit - Miracles, Mystery, Magic

The Holy Spirit is an energy where miracles are born. It is one component of God in the Holy Trinity. The Trinity is Father God, Son Jesus, and The Holy Spirit.

The Holy spirit is that part of us that is connected to the Divine. It is our connection to each other. It is our Higher Self.

Jesus was conceived by the Power of the Holy Spirit and born of the Virgin Mother Mary. The Holy Spirit was present with Jesus during his life and after His death and resurrection and now with His ascension into Heaven.

Miracles happen for those who believe. Ask the Holy Spirit for what you need.

What do you need?

_____

_____

_____

_____

_____

_____

_____

_____

_____

_____

_____

_____

_____

_____

Goddesses

Definition of a Goddess according to Wikipedia is this:

> A **goddess** is a female deity. Goddesses have been linked with virtues such as beauty, love, motherhood and fertility.

What does the word **Goddess** mean to you?

_____

_____

_____

_____

_____

_____

_____

_____

_____

_____

_____

_____

_____

_____

_____

_____

_____

_____

_____

_____

Mother Mary – Mother of Jesus

Goddess whose healing qualities are self love, love and peace.

She is the spiritual embodiment of unconditional love. She helps us learn to fill our own cup and then give from the overflow.

She teaches us to never feel obligated when doing something. Instead do it because you want to and with an open heart.

How does obligation feel to you?

_____

_____

_____

_____

_____

_____

_____

_____

_____

_____

_____

_____

_____

_____

_____

_____

_____

_____

_____

_____

Do you feel worthy of receiving love? Do you have issues with feeling enough? Have you had a great relationship with your birth mother? Or other mother figures in your physical life? Have you a wounded heart due to painful female relationships?

The beautiful beloved Mother Mary is a pure Divine Energy that is available to all of us. She is compassionate, nurturing and protective of all of her children on earth. You can call upon her to open your heart to healing. She is the Mother of Jesus Christ and is our Divine Mother. She is Queen of all the angelic realms.

Mother Mary helps heal all wounds of those adopted or abandoned or in foster care. She is pure unconditional love. She helps you trust that love can be very beautiful.

To invoke her all you have to say is, "Mother Mary, please be a mother to me. I am in need of help. Thank you and so it is."

When her energy is around, you may smell roses as that is her predominate sign. She also sends lady bugs and droplets of water when it is not raining.

With her energy it is safe to expect a miracle. They happen for those who believe. She wants you to have Faith. She hears your prayers and answers are forthcoming. She is trustworthy guidance and support. She is the light that strengthens us in our hearts and souls.

Our beloved mother has various sites around the world where she has been seen. Three such sites are:

1. Fatima - Portugal
2. Lourdes - France
3. Guadalupe – Mexico

Many people travel there to experience her energy and the healing powers of the waters found there. May 13 is a date that we remember her. It is her FEAST day. Commemorating her sighting in Fatima on May 13, 1917.

I have always loved her and I have often asked her for help in my life's journey. My husband and I asked her help to conceive our son. He is now 18! He is our miracle that she promises. I am living proof of her help.

In 2011, when I was diagnosed with cancer, my mom lived in another province and wasn't able to spend long periods of time with me, so it was Mother Mary who nurtured me and loved me and helped me survive. My mom also had her own journey to live and ran for mayor. I had to rely on the help of the Divine Mother.

As I healed from the disease in my body and as I healed my soul I counted on her more and more. I asked her for help in my marriage and for the healing of my son who manifested epilepsy during my chemo days. I know her love. There is nothing you could ever do or ever have done that she will not love you unconditionally.

Mother Mary loves to help small children, and when asked, she will help teachers and healers in their jobs with children. After I was healed and ready to go back to work, I realized I had grown and evolved my soul and my old job was no longer a fit. I had to leave a career in healthcare after 32 years. I felt guided to take a certified angel card reader and angel intuitive course and a mind, body, spirit certification. I also took my Reiki levels 1 and 2.

I fell in love with the Doreen Virtue - Mary Queen of Angels Oracle Cards. As I do readings with this deck, I learn more and more about her and her gentle loving energy. She provides the most beautiful readings of love, support, guidance and inspiration.

SIGNS

I watch for, notice, and trust the signs that heaven continuously sends.

She sends us all a message to pay close attention to the signs that come to you in answer to your prayers.

These can include a song that you hear, words that you read, a sight that you see, a conversation you overhear, and so forth - the possibilities are unlimited.

Signs tend to repeat themselves until you notice them and take some form of action. However, it is also possible to notice one the first time it presents itself.

As you listen to these signs, you get a sense of heaven's continuous participation in your life, which helps you feel safer and more loved.

You can also pray for clarification if you don't understand a sign.

After all, Mother Mary and the angels want to clearly communicate their love to you.

Some signs come in numbers.

Here is what the numbers mean:

    0- God is sending angels to help you
    1- Keep your thoughts positive: Make a wish!
    2- Answered prayers
    3- The Ascended Masters are with you now
    4- Strong presence of the angels
    5- Big happy changes
    6- Quit worrying
    7- You are on the right path
    8- Abundance is flowing to you
    9- Get to work lightworker

You can receive any of these numbers in sequences such as 11, 111, 1111, 22, etc.

What number sequences do you often see? Use the chart above to record their meaning:

Number: **Meaning:**

_____   _____

_____   _____

_____   _____

_____   _____

_____   _____

_____   _____

_____   _____

_____   _____

"She opened herself up to help with Goddess energy and in turn found a Goddess within her. She then turned up her internal flame and burned away the old to welcome the new. She recognized she was a magnificent creation of God and so she straightened her invisible crown and shined brighter than she ever had before."

~Giuliana Melo

Make a list of six things that you love about yourself:

1._____

2._____

3._____

4._____

5._____

6._____

What does self-love mean to me?

_____

_____

_____

_____

_____

_____

_____

_____

_____

_____

_____

_____

_____

_____

_____

_____

PRACTICE

What activities do you do to fill up your cup?

_____
_____
_____
_____
_____
_____
_____
_____
_____
_____
_____
_____

What symptoms do you feel when your cup is empty?

_____
_____
_____
_____
_____
_____
_____
_____
_____
_____
_____
_____

What tools have you learned that you can put in place to help love yourself to health?

_____

_____

_____

_____

_____

_____

_____

How will you continue to practice self-care in your daily life?

_____

_____

_____

_____

_____

_____

_____

_____

_____

_____

_____

_____

_____

Gratitude

Gratitude helped me recognize all my blessings. It turns what we have into enough. Let's count our blessings…

Today I am grateful for:

_____

_____

_____

_____

_____

_____

_____

_____

_____

_____

_____

_____

_____

_____

_____

_____

_____

_____

_____

_____

_____

_____

_____

_____

_____

_____

_____

_____

_____

Today I am grateful for:

Today I am grateful for:

_____

_____

_____

_____

_____

_____

_____

_____

_____

_____

_____

_____

_____

_____

_____

_____

_____

_____

_____

_____

_____

_____

_____

_____

_____

_____

_____

Today I am grateful for:

Today I am grateful for:

_____

_____

_____

_____

_____

_____

_____

_____

_____

_____

_____

_____

_____

_____

_____

_____

_____

_____

_____

_____

_____

_____

_____

_____

_____

_____

_____

Today I am grateful for:

Today I am grateful for:

_____

_____

_____

_____

_____

_____

_____

_____

_____

_____

_____

_____

_____

_____

_____

_____

_____

_____

_____

_____

_____

_____

_____

_____

_____

_____

_____

_____

Today I am grateful for:

_____

_____

_____

_____

_____

_____

_____

_____

_____

_____

_____

_____

_____

_____

_____

_____

_____

_____

_____

_____

_____

_____

_____

_____

_____

_____

_____

_____

_____

_____

Today I am grateful for:

"I admire people who choose to smile after all the things they have been through."

~unknown

Today I am grateful for:

Today I am grateful for:

_____

_____

_____

_____

_____

_____

_____

_____

_____

_____

_____

_____

_____

_____

_____

_____

_____

_____

_____

_____

_____

_____

_____

_____

_____

_____

_____

Today I am grateful for:

_____

_____

_____

_____

_____

_____

_____

_____

_____

_____

_____

_____

_____

_____

_____

_____

_____

_____

_____

_____

_____

_____

_____

_____

_____

_____

_____

Today I am grateful for:

_____

_____

_____

_____

_____

_____

_____

_____

_____

_____

_____

_____

_____

_____

_____

_____

_____

_____

_____

_____

_____

_____

_____

_____

_____

_____

Today I am grateful for:

_____

_____

_____

_____

_____

_____

_____

_____

_____

_____

_____

_____

_____

_____

_____

_____

_____

_____

_____

_____

_____

_____

_____

_____

_____

Today I am grateful for:

_____

_____

_____

_____

_____

_____

_____

_____

_____

_____

_____

_____

_____

_____

_____

_____

_____

_____

_____

_____

_____

_____

_____

_____

_____

_____

_____

_____

Today I am grateful for:

_____

_____

_____

_____

_____

_____

_____

_____

_____

_____

_____

_____

_____

_____

_____

_____

_____

_____

_____

_____

_____

_____

_____

_____

_____

_____

_____

_____

_____

_____

Today I am grateful for:

Today I am grateful for:

_____

_____

_____

_____

_____

_____

_____

_____

_____

_____

_____

_____

_____

_____

_____

_____

_____

_____

_____

_____

_____

_____

_____

_____

_____

_____

_____

Today I am grateful for:

Today I am grateful for:

"When an illness is a part of your spiritual journey, no medical intervention can heal you until your spirit has begun to make the changes that the illness was designed to inspire."

~ Carolyn Myss

Today I am grateful for:

_____

_____

_____

_____

_____

_____

_____

_____

_____

_____

_____

_____

_____

_____

_____

_____

_____

_____

_____

_____

_____

_____

_____

_____

_____

_____

_____

_____

Today I am grateful for:

_____

_____

_____

_____

_____

_____

_____

_____

_____

_____

_____

_____

_____

_____

_____

_____

_____

_____

_____

_____

_____

_____

_____

_____

_____

_____

_____

_____

Today I am grateful for:

_____

_____

_____

_____

_____

_____

_____

_____

_____

_____

_____

_____

_____

_____

_____

_____

_____

_____

_____

_____

_____

_____

_____

_____

_____

_____

Today I am grateful for:

_____

_____

_____

_____

_____

_____

_____

_____

_____

_____

_____

_____

_____

_____

_____

_____

_____

_____

_____

_____

_____

_____

_____

_____

_____

_____

_____

_____

_____

Today I am grateful for:

_____

_____

_____

_____

_____

_____

_____

_____

_____

_____

_____

_____

_____

_____

_____

_____

_____

_____

_____

_____

_____

_____

_____

_____

_____

_____

_____

Today I am grateful for:

Today I am grateful for:

_____

_____

_____

_____

_____

_____

_____

_____

_____

_____

_____

_____

_____

_____

_____

_____

_____

_____

_____

_____

_____

_____

_____

_____

_____

_____

_____

_____

Today I am grateful for:

Today I am grateful for:

_____

_____

_____

_____

_____

_____

_____

_____

_____

_____

_____

_____

_____

_____

_____

_____

_____

_____

_____

_____

_____

_____

_____

_____

_____

_____

Today I am grateful for:

Today I am grateful for:

_____

_____

_____

_____

_____

_____

_____

_____

_____

_____

_____

_____

_____

_____

_____

_____

_____

_____

_____

_____

_____

_____

_____

_____

_____

_____

_____

_____

_____

Today I am grateful for:

_____

_____

_____

_____

_____

_____

_____

_____

_____

_____

_____

_____

_____

_____

_____

_____

_____

_____

_____

_____

_____

_____

_____

_____

_____

_____

_____

_____

_____

_____

Today I am grateful for:

"We are not alone. We are spirit, embodied. We are connected to Source through the love that we are. Remember, we can heal our lives. We must make a choice to do something that changes our life. The secret is to look at the daily routine. Take a chance on you. You are worth it."

~Giuliana Giuliano-Melo

The Journey Continues...

Giuliana Melo believes in the Divine healing energy of the Universe with her entire being. She loves being of service and connecting others to their Divine team of helpers. She is a fun and faithful angel intuitive who is shining her light and loving life!

Having walked her own journey of cancer and grief, she now supports others through their life struggles with help from God and the angelic realm through angel card readings and angel prayers.

If you are looking for someone who exudes love and makes you feel special and loved, then look no further. She will guide and support you with

- Love

- Support

- Connection to your Divine Team

After her walk through cancer in 2011, she made it her mission in life being of service to others. For the last seven years, she has created a spiritual business to help others on their healing journey and has become a kindness ambassador. With her, you will also have access to many integral spiritual teachers and tribes of support.

With the creation of this workbook, she hopes to help inspire you to bring more self-love into your life. This workbook has been a labour of love, and the culmination of all the work she has done, with all the teachers she has had.

About the Author

In 2011, Giuliana Melo was diagnosed with stage 3 cancer of the peritoneum, with metastases to the uterus, cervix, ovaries, tubes and appendix. In a moment in her anger she cried out to God and asked, Why me? In that moment she heard the voice of God reply, "Why not you, Giuliana?" She then realized that she had to surrender the will of her life to God and ask for help. She tuned in to her intuition and began to follow her spirit. She allowed the Divine Healing of the Universe to help propel her on her road of healing.

She was born and raised in Fernie BC and moved to Calgary in 1982. She went to SAIT and attained her certificate in Health Information Management. She was blessed to have worked for Alberta Health Services for thirty-two years; however, after her journey through cancer she realized she wanted to pursue her love of all things Divine. Giuliana has been married for thirty-one years to a wonderful man and has a twenty-year-old son. She loves and lives in Calgary AB Canada.

Today she helps others cultivate self-love and live their truth. She can be reached for angel card sessions at **www.giulianamelo.com**

Heal with Giuliana

Made in the USA
San Bernardino, CA
29 November 2018